Ballerina Poems

Clare ⸱⸱⸱ n lives in a cobwebby house with
her h⸱⸱⸱ nd, Martin, her son, Ben, and a
rathe⸱ ⸱⸱⸱ m⸱⸱⸱ ⸱⸱⸱ed cat called Myfanwy.
She ⸱⸱⸱ ⸱⸱⸱ut now she spends
mos⸱ ⸱⸱⸱ Her favourite
hob⸱ ⸱⸱⸱ and riding
aro⸱ ⸱⸱⸱ tricycle.

Lar⸱ ⸱⸱⸱ age by a misty hill
with⸱ ⸱⸱⸱ She likes painting
pictu⸱ ⸱⸱⸱ on toast and day
dream⸱

Other books from Macmillan

FAIRY POEMS
By Clare Bevan
Illustrated by Lara Jones

PRINCESS POEMS
By Clare Bevan
Illustrated by Lara Jones

MERMAID POEMS
By Clare Bevan
Illustrated by Lara Jones

CRAZY MAYONNAISY MUM
By Julia Donaldson
Illustrated by Nick Sharratt

Ballerina Poems

By Clare Bevan

Illustrated by Lara Jones

MACMILLAN CHILDREN'S BOOKS

First published 2007 by Macmillan Children's Books
a division of Macmillan Publishers Limited
20 New Wharf Road, London N1 9RR
Basingstoke and Oxford
www.panmacmillan.com

Associated companies throughout the world

ISBN: 978-0-230-01542-5

Text copyright © Clare Bevan 2007
Illustrations copyright © Lara Jones 2007

3 5 7 9 8 6 4 2

A CIP catalogue record for this book is available from
the British Library.

Typeset by Nigel Hazle
Printed and bound in Great Britain by Mackays of Chatham plc, Kent

For the little cygnets
who read this book –
may you all become
beautiful swans

C. B.

For India, my
little ballerina

L. J.

Contents

Names for a Dancer

This list was found inside an old book of ballet stories.

Names for a dancer
Who swirls on the stage
Need to be FRISKY, whatever her age.

Kate? Or Carlotta?
Or sweet Antoinette?
Names that are happy and hard to forget.

Samira? Maria?
Tamara? You choose.
Names that are light as a pair of pink shoes.

Ravenna? Or Darcey?
Or Petra perhaps?
Names you can murmur while everyone claps.

Small Angelina?
Or Anna the Swan?
Names that paint pictures when
everyone's gone.

Margo? Miranda?
Or Fifi? Let's find
Names that make music in everyone's
mind.

Names for a dancer
Should sparkle and fizz . . .
And YOUR name is perfect, whatever it is.

Most of these names belong to real ballet stars.

The Best Bits

Clare's favourite bit is the plate of pink butterfly cakes at the end of the lesson.

The best bits of ballet,

The bits that I love,

Are: my silkiest

Slippers, as soft

As a glove,

My sparkly hairgrips, my sequins

That shine, my boxes of make-up, my ribbons that twine,

But mostly my T U T U. It's P I N K.
And it's M I N E !!

How to Tie a Ballet Shoe

This poem was tied with a silky, pink ribbon.

Take a ribbon,
Make your ribbon
Flick and flow,
Twine around and
Wind around
And don't be slow,
Curl about and
Furl about and
Don't let go.

Second ribbon,
Swing the rhythm
To and fro,
Left and right and
Tie it tight and
Lean down low,
Cut the ends and
Tuck the ends and
Point your toe.

The Arabesque

Real ballerinas balance on one foot while they say this poem.

I'll now explain
THE ARABESQUE –
A tricky word that
Rhymes with DESK,
But means (I know
It seems absurd)
A movement rather
Like a bird . . .

Your arms are held
Like two small wings,
One leg is raised
(As if on strings)
The other foot must
Touch the ground,
Before you spin
Around, around . . .

And if you twist
With style and grace
(Don't fall upon
Your knees. Or face.)
The crowd will clap
And cheer – and then
You'll have to do it
  ALL AGAIN!

Tuesday's Child

In the old nursery rhyme, Tuesday's child is full of grace.

Her skirt is green. Her name is Grace.
She puffs some powder on her face.

She ties her hair with silver strings.
She wears a pair of painted wings.

She knows her solo off by heart.
She waits to hear the music start.

Her smile is wide. Her dance begins.
She flicks her head. Her wheelchair spins.

She swoops and swerves with shining eyes,
Then flutters with the butterflies.

While, in the middle of the crowd,
Her Gran and Grandad look SO proud.

A Counting Rhyme for Bedtime Ballerinas

This poem will help you dream about your FAVOURITE ballet.

ONE –   You twist your feet aside,

TWO –   You place them neat and wide.

THREE – You cross one foot halfway –
        Do not wobble! Do not sway!

FOUR – You turn both feet about –
        Leave a space and do not pout.

FIVE – You wait a little while,
        Touch and cross and try to
            smile.

SIX –   You add your hands, knees,
            thumbs,
        Practise all your Ballet Sums,
        Learn the things a dancer
            knows –

AND

SEVEN – You'll spin upon your toes.

Find That Fairy!

Clare found this puzzle inside her Christmas stocking.

My first is in SWEETS and also in SPICE,
My second's in MOUSE but not in MICE,
My third is in GIRL but not in BOY,
My fourth is in CRACKER but not in TOY,
My fifth is in DREAMS but not in SLEEP.

My sixth is in PRESENT and also PEEP,
My seventh's in CLARA but not in
      COFFEE,
My eighth is in NUTSHELL but not in
      TOFFEE,
My last is in CHRISTMAS but not in
      TREE,
And my ALL is the Fairy I'd like to be.

Answer:

Nibble every clue and crumb –
Then you'll find the SUGAR PLUM!

Lily-May

Is there someone in YOUR ballet class who is a bit like Lily-May?

An elephant joined our lesson today
(She's AWFULLY keen, and she's called
    Lily-May).
She pointed her trunk in the daintiest way,
Then she squashed all the girls in the corps
    de ballet.

She started to trumpet a jungly beat,
She tripped on her slippers, she trampled
    our feet,
She sat on the cakes we were hoping to eat
(But she's called Lily-May, and she's
    AWFULLY sweet).

Ballet Bag

Clare seems to have trouble finding ANYTHING in her ballet bag.

In my ballet bag you'll find . . .

Two long ribbons neatly twined;
Sparkly hairgrips (just in case);
Pots of powder for my face;
A sewing kit, some spare elastic;
A comb of pink and shiny plastic;
A silky flower from a friend;
A sock I really need to mend;
My satin slippers, tightly packed;

A tiny mirror (slightly cracked);
A tape of ballet tunes to play;

A cygnet feather, soft and grey;
My lucky charm (a silver shoe);
A floaty scarf (it's green and blue);
A Darcey Bussell photo (signed!)

At least – that's what I HOPE you'll find.

Ten Little Bumblebees

Clare hopes these little dancers didn't get into too much trouble.

> Ten little bumblebees
> Fidget and fumble,
> Wait in the wings with
> A buzz and a mumble:

"We'll try not to stamp and we'll try not to
    stumble,
Or tipple or topple, or tangle or tumble,
Or get in a muddle or huddle or jumble,
Or thunder or blunder, or make the stage
    rumble . . .

        Our parents won't mind –
        But Miss Grimble will
        GRUMBLE!"

The Littlest Dancer

Clare found this poem in the littlest dancer's shoe bag.

The littlest dancer – she waves at the
   crowd.
She giggles and wriggles. She's terribly
   loud.
She twiddles her hair when she's meant to
   look proud.

The littlest dancer – she misses her cues.
She trips on her ribbons. She scuffles her
   shoes.
She nibbles her fingers and points at a
   bruise.

The littlest dancer – she won't wear her
   beak.
She won't do the part that she practised
   last week.
She drops all her props with a BANG and
   a squeak.

The littlest dancer – she's simply a pest,
She shouts as she tramples her socks and
    her vest –
"The others are bigger – but I am the
    BEST!"

Miss Miranda and Miss Grey

Clare once knew a teacher who was as beautiful as Miss Miranda and as kind as old Miss Grey.

Miss Miranda's beautiful,
Her hair gleams like the moon,
Her back is straight as poplar trees
(Miss Grey just plays the tune).

Miss Miranda's elegant,
She slinks like midnight cats,
She wears a skirt of silver mist
(Miss Grey wears woolly hats).

Miss Miranda's dazzling,
She darts like summer bees,
Her fingers zigzag through the air
(Miss Grey just hits the keys).

Miss Miranda's magical,
Her voice is crispy sweet,
She fills our minds with dancing dreams
(Miss Grey just taps her feet).

Miss Miranda's marvellous,
A soaring, sunlit dove,
And she's the one we want to be
(Miss Grey's the one we love).

Little Fifi's First Lesson

Clare tries to point her toes, but they just WON'T behave.

Little Fifi tries her best
In her frilly skirt and vest.

Tries to place her feet just so.
Tries to curtsy neat and low.
Tries to point her toes with style.
Tries to lift her chin and smile.
Tries to be a swooping bird.
Tries to follow every word.
Tries to copy this and that –
Arabesque and "entrechat".
Tries to pick a magic flower.
Tries and TRIES for one whole hour.
Tries to dance like me. And you.

But ballet steps are hard to do –
And Little Fifi's only two!

The Big Mirror

When Clare is by herself, she looks in the Big Mirror and pretends to be a famous ballerina.

Here we are – the short, the tall.
There's the mirror – one whole wall!

MOST of us stand still and straight.
ONE girl's just a moment late.
MOST of us look calm and neat.
ONE girl muddles up her feet.
MOST of us stretch high, sweep low.
ONE girl's stiff and rather slow.
MOST of us skip fast then stop.
ONE girl makes an extra hop.
MOST of us turn right and stay.
ONE girl twists the other way.
MOST of us spin more and more.
ONE girl tumbles on the floor.

MOST of us race home for tea,
But in the mirror I can see
ONE girl's waving. Look – it's ME!

Ballet Limericks

Ballet is meant to be beautiful – but sometimes funny things happen.

1. A small ballet star from Australia
   Danced as a doll in *Coppelia* –
   She tripped on the toys,
   Made a terrible noise,
   And her curtsy (KER-SPLATT!) was
      a failure.

2. A lively young dancer called Lizzy
   Was always a little too fizzy,
   She twizzled until
   She was told to stand still –
   Then grumbled because she felt dizzy.

3. A sniffly dancer from Chertsey
   Attempted a sweet little curtsy –
   She started to sneeze,
   Which created a breeze,
   And she flew like a kite in her skirtsy.

4. "Imagine," my dance teacher said,
   "A spider hung over your head."
   But that was so scary
   And horribly hairy . . .
   I dangled a doughnut instead!

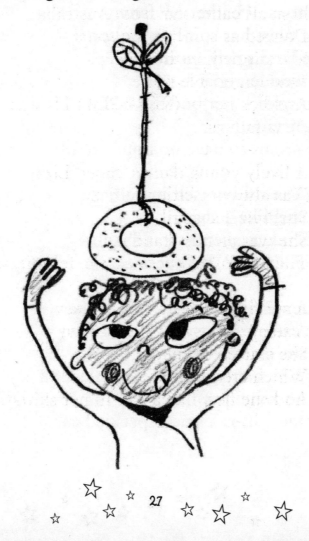

The Backyard Ballerina

Clare says that Myfanwy is the BEST ballerina she knows.

Light-as-a-feather Myfanwy
Can twist her spine as she spins,
Can land softly on stone steps
Or wooden boards.
Can stretch her body so lazily,
So curvily
She seems to have no bones at all.

She can fold herself in half,
Or curl like a snail,
Or slink as silently as a shadow
Over, around, between.

In her dreams,
She can swoop with the sparrows
Across the wide stage of the sky,
But when she gazes at her reflection
In the green pool,
All she sees is a small speckled cat

With damp whiskers
And dancing eyes.

*"Myfanwy" is a Welsh name. It sounds like
"miff-AN-wee" and it means "My fine one".*

Left Right

Clare has odd-sized feet, and BOTH of them are clumsy.

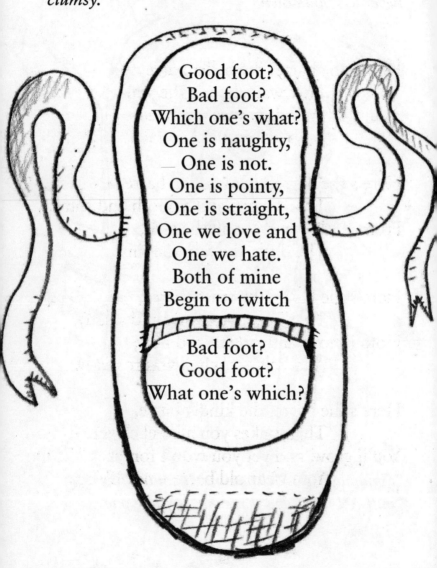

Good foot?
Bad foot?
Which one's what?
One is naughty,
One is not.
One is pointy,
One is straight,
One we love and
One we hate.
Both of mine
Begin to twitch

Bad foot?
Good foot?
What one's which?

The Barre

The barre doesn't look exciting – but it never lets you down!

Here's the barre, the ballet barre
      That waits beside the wall.
A faithful friend, it does not bend,
      And will not let you fall.

Here's the barre, the wooden barre
      That's worn and smooth and shiny,
From all the twirls of all the girls,
      The dark, the fair, the tiny.

Here's the barre, the trusty barre,
      That's always strong and steady,
Hold it now, and stretch and bow,
      And balance when you're ready.

Here's the barre, the kindly barre,
      That makes you all feel clever.
You'll grow, and yet you won't forget
      Your dear old barre – not EVER.

Try, Try, Try Again

Really clever dancers can spin without feeling dizzy, but Clare hasn't learned the trick yet.

My teacher said to try a step
I'd never tried before.
I tried to dance a pirouette . . .
I flipped and hit the floor.
So she said:
"Try again and
Try again and
Try a little more."

My teacher said to try a step
That made me shake with fear.
I tried to dance a pirouette . . .
I tripped and banged my ear.
So she said:
"Try again and
Try again and
Try again, my dear."

My teacher said to try a step
That's tricky as can be.
I tried to dance a pirouette . . .
I slipped and bumped my knee.
So she said:
"Try again and
Try again and
Try once more for me."

I tried again,
I tried again . . .
And did it EASILY!

Petunia's Ballet School Report

*Clare found this little poem underneath
a cuddly polar bear.*

Petunia is NOT a star.
She wobbles when she holds the barre.
Her steps are neither swift nor neat.
She tends to flap and slap her feet.
She CANNOT balance on one leg
(She looks as if she's laid an egg)!
Her warm-up takes her FAR too long.
Her tutu dangles – which is WRONG.
In class, I know she tries her best,
She always wears a clean white vest.
Her smiles are sweet, but when she skips
She loses ribbons, pins and grips,
And in her test she sneezed and fell . . .

But (for a PENGUIN) she does well.

Signed:

Madame SnowLady

The Little Cygnets

*Clare found this poem wrapped around
a fluffy grey feather.*

All the little cygnets
                Are dancing in a line,
Feathers softly whisper,
                Fingers gently twine.

All the girls are beautiful.
                All the girls are clever.
Most of them will dance beside
                The magic lake forever.

One will change into a swan
                And play the finest part –
But she will meet a handsome prince,
                And he will break her heart.

A Dazzle of Dancers

This poem was pinned to a page of piano music.

A Worry of Teachers
Who tidy our hair.
A Quiver of Music
That tickles the air.
A Rustle of Tutus.
A Tiptoe of Shoes.
A Shiver of Petticoats
(Pale pinks and blues).

A Scamper of Children.
A Scurry of Mice.
A Whirlwind of Villains
With smiles cold as ice.
A Snowstorm of Cygnets
Who flutter together.
A Sorrow of Swans
(They can float like a feather).

A Gallop of Hunters
Who race round the stage.
A Frown of Bad Fairies
Who stamp and who rage.
A Dazzle of Dancers
Who try not to fall,
                    AND
A Gather of Grown-Ups –
(They're proud of us ALL).

On Pointe

Clare can't dance on pointe, but she's VERY good at wobbling.

On pointe –
That's where I want to go,
Poised upon one magic toe,
Not a wobble, not a lurch,
Still as statues in a church.

Arms raised high and eyes cast low,
Dressed in feathers white as snow,
Not a flicker, not a shake,
Motionless beside the lake.
Round about the stage I'll glide
While the moonlit cygnets hide,
Not a stumble, not a sway,
I'll be there ON POINTE some day.

Dear Firebird

(A fan letter)

Have you ever written a fan letter to your FAVOURITE dancer? If you are lucky, they might write back to YOU.

Dear Firebird,

You dazzle
You spiral and burn,
You flicker your fingers.
You suddenly turn
To sizzle the monsters,
To spin from their trap –
You are the Firebird.
I gaze and I clap.

Your costume is scarlet
And ragged as flame,
You're fierce as a firework,
Your dance is a game
To tease the Magician,

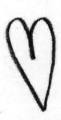

To smoulder and swirl –
You are the Firebird.
And I'm a small girl.

But when you were little,
When you were my age,
Did YOU watch a dancer
Who whirled on the stage?
Did YOU wish for feathers
All sparky and wild –
When she was the Firebird,
And you were the child?

x x x x x x

Kitty and Evie and India Rose

(For Gaby and Lara)

This poem came fluttering out of a book of ballet poems.

Look at the ballet girls
Pointing their toes –
Kitty and Evie and India Rose.

Who'll be the Princess
So sleepy and pretty?
Will it be India, Evie or Kitty?

Who'll be the Fairy
Who has the most fun?
India, Kitty or Evie? Which one?

Who'll be the Cat
With the painted pink nose?
Evie or Kitty or India Rose?

And who'll wear a gown
At the glittering ball?
(I'll tell you a secret – I've chosen them
    ALL.)

Pas de Deux

A Pas de Deux is a dance for two people –
and in this poem even the words and
verses come in pairs!

1. Em holds
   My hand –
   It's our
   Big Night . . .
   Oh dear,
   Oh dear,
   We shake
   With fright.

2. At last
   We hear
   Our ting-
   Tang-tune . . .
   Oh dear,
   Oh dear,
   We've twirled
   Too soon.

3. Some steps
   Are short
   Some steps
   Are long . . .
   Oh dear,
   Oh dear,
   We've both
   Gone wrong.

4. We must
   Keep close,
   We must
   Take care . . .
   Oh dear,
   Oh dear,
   I'm here,
   Em's there.

5. We must
   Not stamp
   Or flap
   Our feet . . .
   Oh dear,
   Oh dear,
   We've lost
   The beat.

6. And now
   Our Pas
   De Deux
   Must end . . .
   Oh dear,
   Oh dear,
   I've tripped
   My friend.

7. The mums
   And dads
   Don't cheer
   Or clap . . .
   Oh dear,
   Oh dear,
   Their hands
   Just flap.

8. They wipe
   Their eyes
   On sleeve
   And scarf . . .
   Oh dear,
   Oh dear,
   We've made
   Them LAUGH!

Entrechat

*Clare tried to do an entrechat, but she crossed
when she should have crissed.*

Entrechat,
Pitter pat,
Whisper it sweetly,
Cross your feet,
Criss your feet,
Touch the floor neatly.

Bounce and fly,
Brush the sky,
Smile very brightly.
Criss your feet,
Cross your feet,
Land again lightly.

The Ballet Test

Clare always feels nervous before a test. Do you?

My test is tomorrow,
I'm trying to sleep,
I'm closing my eyes and
I'm counting pink sheep . . .
They're all dressed in tutus!
The night slowly spins.
I must pack my mirror,
My comb and my pins.

My test will be over
In less than an hour.
I'm trying to sniff
An invisible flower,
I'm trying to ripple
My delicate hands,
And gaze at the shells
On invisible sands.

My test is beginning
In less than a minute.
My tummy feels odd –
There are elephants in it!
I'm trying to keep myself
Tidy and neat,
As I ruffle my skirt
And I turn out my feet.

My test is all over.
I tried not to laugh
When Mia fell over and
May dropped her scarf.
But now I can wriggle
And giggle at last . . .
MY TEST IS ALL OVER.
(I hope that I passed.)

The Boy Who Plays the Bluebird

Clare would love to go to Princess Aurora's wedding party – and dance with the Bluebird. Perhaps he could teach her how to fly!

Everybody talks about the boys who
 charge about;
The boys who like to wrestle;
The boys who like to shout.
Everybody talks about the boys who fight
 and fall . . .
But the boy who plays the Bluebird –
He's the STRONGEST of them all.

Everybody talks about the boys who leap
 around;
The boys who win the high jump;
The boys who race and bound.
Everybody talks about the boys who kick a
 ball . . .
But the boy who plays the Bluebird –
He's the BOUNCIEST of all.

Everybody talks about the boys who play
    guitars;
The boys who think they're clever;
The boys who think they're stars.
Everybody talks about the boys who fill
    the hall . . .
But the boy who plays the Bluebird –
He's the best, THE BEST OF ALL.

Ten Timid Dancers

Clare thinks the Wishful Dancer will be a dazzling Firebird one day.

Ten –	Timid dancers waiting to begin,
Nine –	Naughty dancers trying not to grin,
Eight –	Achy dancers rubbing tired toes,
Seven –	Spooky dancers wearing cobweb clothes,
Six –	Swirly dancers whirling in a ring,
Five –	Frilly dancers skipping past a King,
Four –	Frisky dancers, frolicsome and fizzy,
Three –	Thoughtful dancers feeling rather dizzy,
Two –	Tidy dancers pinning back their hair,

AND . . .

One –	Wishful dancer spinning through the air.

The Skeleton Ballet

A skeleton ballet would probably be DREADFULLY noisy!

There's a jiggle and a wiggle
At the Skeleton Ballet –

There's a shiver and a quiver
As the band begins to play,

There's a clatter and a scatter
As the leg-bones start to sway,

There's a rattle and a battle
As the hairbands go astray,

There's a tumble and a jumble
As the dancers skip away,

And a clapping and a slapping
As the ghosties shout, "Hooray!"

Bad Hair Day

Clare has an awful lot of Bad Hair Days.

I'm washing my,
Squashing my
Straggly hair,
I'm patting it,
Plaiting it,
Taking great care.

I'm shrugging it,
Tugging it
Back from my face
I'm brushing it,
Crushing it
Smoothly in place.

I'm clipping it,
Gripping it,
Pinning it tight.
I shan't let it,
Can't let it,
Tangle tonight.

I grin at it,
Spin a bit,
Skip in the rain,
I drizzle it,
Frizzle it . . .
START IT AGAIN!

The Little Dancer

*Would you like an artist to make a tiny statue of
YOU in your best tutu?*

Degas painted ballet girls.
He made a statue too –
And still the Little Dancer points
Her dainty satin shoe.

The girl who touched the painter's heart
Grew old. The fast years flew.
Yet still her statue stands as brave
And young, my child, as you.

*Degas was a French artist, so his name rhymes
with 'Day-Star'.*

Beautiful Dreamer

This poem was hidden underneath Clare's pillow.

I'll never be
A ballet girl –

I stumble when I want to swirl
I can't keep time (although I try),
My skirts won't float, my shoes won't tie,
I watch the others rustle by,
Then pack my tutu with a sigh . . .

But in my dreams, the people cry:
"Oh, where's the dancer small and shy,
Who seems to sparkle, seems to fly
Like fireworks through the starry sky?
The girl who's frisky as can be . . ."

The spotlight shines –
That girl is ME!

The Insect Orchestra

Clare once saw a moon moth – and the tips of its pearly wings looked just like tiny ballet shoes.

In a lost corner of the sleepy wood,
Where stars paint golden circles
On the tangled grass,
A curtain of cobwebs swings back
And the Insect Orchestra starts to play . . .
Tssk, tssk.
Chee, chee,
Hmmmm.

Now the moon moths begin their summer
    ballet.
They spin and spiral among the leaves,
They balance on beams of light
And their pale tendrils tiptoe
Like satin shoes,
As the Insect Orchestra trills and buzzes
Tssk, tssk.
Chee, chee,
Hmmmm.

Lines of silver midges form a glittering
    necklace
As a solo bat swoops
Impossibly high,
Impossibly low,
And the Insect Orchestra chirps and
    whines
Faster, faster . . .
Tssk, tssk.
Chee, chee,
Hmmmm.

Then the glow-worms blink
The cobwebs fall,
And all the tiny dancers whirl away
Until only the Insect Orchestra is left
To sigh and remember
And troop home . . .
Tssk, tssk.
Chee, chee,
Hmmmm.

Ragged-Claw and Starlight

Clare's old cat used to yowl just like
Ragged-Claw.

Ragged-Claw yowls like a wild concertina,
He scratches a rackety tune,
While Starlight the cat (a divine ballerina)
Appears in the beams of the moon.

She silkily crawls along fences and walls,
She swishes her tail to and fro,
She twists on her paws and she expertly
    falls
While Ragged-Claw wails far below.

The garden mice tiptoe and twirl on the
    lawn,
They vanish away one by one,
While Starlight spins daintily into the
    dawn
And Ragged-Claw yawns at the sun.

The Bus-Stop Dancer

Clare wishes she had seen the Bus-Stop Ballerina.

The old lady at the bus stop
Puts down her big, bulgy bag,
Looks this way,
That way,
And lifts her arms towards the moon.

Then, dainty as a moth,
She skips around the broken seat
To place one cold hand
On its rusty rail.

Slowly, very slowly,
She raises her left foot
In its brown boot
And suddenly she is twirling
Like a girl,
Like the little ballerina
She used to be.

When the bus wheezes by
She turns back into her sensible self.
She stumps aboard
With her bag and her boots
And grumbles away into the darkness.

No one knows her secret.
Only a quiet camera
Fixed to the concrete wall
Blinks its astonished eye
And turns to watch her go.

Madame de la Mare's Ballet School

This ballet school is under the sea!

Madame de la Mare
Balances on the very tip
Of her pale pink tail,
Peers over her pink spectacles
And waits for silence.

The little mermaids point their fins.
They try SO hard
Not to wobble
As the music begins,
And Madame beats time
With her sea-urchin spike.

"First position!" she calls
Ten tails flick left.
"Second." They flick to the right.
"Third." A whirl.
"Fourth." A swirl.
"Fifth." A flutter of the fingers.
"And sixth." Most difficult of all.

A corkscrew spin, up, up,
Into the starlight
With wide-open eyes
And not even the smallest splutter
Or splash.

Now the little mermaids tumble
Dizzily down
In a giggling whirlpool
And flap their tails
On the sandy floor.

Madame de la Mare claps her hands
To make her silver rings jingle.
"Bravo," she cries.
"Well spun, my children."
And she rewards her clumsy ballerinas
With a rare and glittering smile.

Tutu

When Clare dances, she looks a bit like the little hippo.

Behold the Hippo, shy and sweet,
Satin slippers on her feet,
Twirling to a dreamy beat.

Does her tutu seem too small?
Does she sometimes trip and fall?
Does her head-dress slip at all?

Does it matter? There she goes,
Hopeful as a morning rose,
Spinning on her happy toes.

Giselle

Clare quite likes scary stories – do you?

The spookiest tale with the scariest spell
  And the ghastliest ghosts
  Is the one called *Giselle*.

  There's a horrible queen
  In a cobwebby crown,
  There's a sorrowful girl
  In a shadowy gown,
  There's a poor boy to pity,
  A rich boy to save,
  There's a rosebud that lies
  On a faraway grave.

One ballet is sadder than all of the rest –
GISELLE makes me cry – and I like it the
  best.

Sugar Plum

Do you sometimes wish you could be the Sugar Plum Fairy?

Oh, the Sugar Plum Fairy
So sweet and so airy –
THAT'S who I'm hoping to be.
I'll gracefully fly
Past the painted blue sky
As light as a leaf on a tree.

In my Sugar Plum dress,
Like a story princess,
I'll scatter my magical charms.
I'll sparkle and glow,
I'll twist on one toe,
I'll flutter my feathery arms.

Oh, my Sugar Plum dance
(If I'm given the chance)
Will make all the other girls say:
"How clever you are!
You're a new ballet star –
And you've just started lessons TODAY."

Aurora

The Sleeping Beauty's name is Aurora. It means "Dawn" and that's why she usually wears sunshine colours.

Aurora, Aurora, the Princess of Dawn,
Cursed by a fairy the day you were born.

Aurora, Aurora, you're loved by us all,
Everyone comes to your beautiful ball.

Aurora, Aurora, beware of the flowers.
Beware of old ladies with magical powers.

Aurora, Aurora, the spindle is found.
Carabosse laughs as you sink to the
 ground.

Aurora, Aurora, the Princess of Sleep,
Years tiptoe by while the brambles grow
    deep.

Aurora, Aurora, there still is a chance
Your prince will appear – and together
    you'll DANCE.

Carabosse is the bad fairy.

Odette and Odile

Usually the same ballerina dances Odile and Odette in Swan Lake – she must have to change her costume very quickly!

Odette and Odile – Odile and Odette,
Both of them lovely and lively, and yet . . .
Odette has a sweet and a sorrowful heart,
Odile has the dark and the dangerous part.

Odette wears white feathers. Odile wears a
    crown
As spiky as holly, as fierce as a frown.
Odette is enchanted. Odile can weave
    charms
To capture a prince in her glittery arms.

One day, if you're lucky, you'll be the sad
    swan
As well as the bad girl who laughs and is
    gone.
Odette's warm and loving, Odile's cold as
    steel
But who is EXCITING? Odette or Odile?

Swanhilda

Swanhilda is the naughty girl in Coppelia *who creeps into the old Toy Maker's house and discovers that Coppelia is just a doll.*

Don't want to be a Sugar Plum
In pretty pink and blue.
Don't want to be a sweet Princess,
Too dainty to be true.
I want to be a village girl
Who's naughty through and through.

Don't want to be a pussy cat
With lipstick on my nose.
Don't want to be a flower girl
Who sniffs a paper rose.
I want to be a crafty girl
Who skips on saucy toes.

Don't want to be Red Riding Hood
Who hides behind a tree.
Don't want to be a little wave
Who ripples like the sea.
I want to be a risky girl
Who's brave as brave can be . . .

SWANHILDA likes to break the rules,
So THAT'S the part for me.

Ballet is . . .

What do YOU think Ballet is . . . ?

Ballet is . . .
Stories without any words.
Girls dressed as snowflakes and roses and
birds.

Ballet is . . .
Sequins and whispery skirts.
Neatly turned feet – and a blister that
hurts!

Ballet is . . .
Practice, when nothing feels right.
A fizz of excitement on opening night.

Ballet is . . .
Ribbons and pins for your hair.
A spangly, dangly costume to wear.

Ballet is . . .
Music, and curtains that swish.
A sunburst of light and a last-minute wish.

Ballet is . . .
Faces, all gazing at YOU.
A dance that is ALMOST too good to be
true.

Ballet is . . .
Balance. The tip of one toe.
Tattered pink shoes at the end of the show.

Ballet is . . .
Curtsies. A long, silent pause.
A moment of worry. A BURST of applause.

Ballet is . . .
Joy when you know you danced well.
Ballet is MAGIC. And YOU cast the spell.

Ballet Stories

Here are a few famous ballet stories, in case you've never heard them before.

1. Giselle

This is a spooky story about a rich boy called Albrecht and a poor boy called Hilarion. They both fall in love with pretty Giselle, but Albrecht can't marry her because she is only a village girl. So Giselle dies of sorrow and becomes one of the ghostly girls who dance with handsome young men until they die! This has already happened to unlucky Hilarion – but Giselle saves Albrecht, and he lives SADLY ever after!

2. Swan Lake

This is a sorrowful story too. One evening Prince Siegfried meets a lovely maiden called Odette, who is under a cruel spell. By day, she and all her friends turn into swans! Of course, the prince falls in love with her and promises to break the spell – but the wicked magician's daughter plays a trick on him. Her name is Odile and she looks EXACTLY like Odette, and Siegfried accidentally asks the wrong girl to marry him. Oh no! Now Odette can never be free, so she and her prince decide to die together in the waters of the lake.

(Everyone hopes their souls will live HAPPILY ever after.)

3. Coppelia

Hooray! This story is FUN. Swanhilda is a village girl who has a boyfriend called Franz – but he has fallen in love with the old Toy Maker's beautiful daughter, Coppelia. So naughty Swanhilda creeps inside the toy shop . . . and discovers that Coppelia is just a DOLL. There's a scary bit, when the old Toy Maker tries to steal Franz's soul, but everything is all right in the end, and all the people enjoy a happy dance in the village square.

4. The Nutcracker

One Christmas, a little girl called Clara is given a strange Nutcracker. It looks just like a soldier, and that night it springs to life. The Nutcracker leads all the other toy soldiers in a battle against an army of bad rats, and Clara throws her slipper at the Rat King. Her reward is a trip to the Kingdom of Sweets, where she meets the Sugar Plum Fairy. But was her adventure real – or was it all a dream?

5. The Firebird

This is a magical ballet story. Prince Ivan traps the Firebird in an enchanted garden, but she gives him a dazzling feather and he sets her free. Later she rescues him from an evil magician, and he marries his favourite princess. I think I like this tale the best of all.

CLARE BEVAN

Fairy Poems

Do you believe in fairies?

These fairy poems were scribbled on stones and tucked under pillows, and they revealed lots of fairy secrets! In this book you will find out where the tooth fairy goes, what naughty fairies like to do for fun and how to sing fairy songs. And don't forget to practise your flying for the fairy ball!

A Bedtime Rhyme for Young Fairies

One tired fairy,
Two folded wings,
Three magic wishes,
Four daisy rings,
Five moonlight dancers,
Six starlight spells,
Seven hidden treasures,
Eight silver bells,
Nine secret doorways,
Ten keys to keep,
And one little fairy
Fast asleep.

CLARE BEVAN

Princess Poems

Could you be a princess?

A gorgeous collection of poems filled with tips on how to
behave like a princess, meet the right prince and avoid the
dangers posed by wicked stepmothers, dragons and unhappy
fairy godmothers.

If You Were a Princess

If YOU were a princess, what would YOU ride?
A small, metal dragon
with cogwheels inside?
A horse with white feathers
and hooves of black glass?
A silvery unicorn
pounding the grass?
A fluttering carpet
that chases the bats?
A big, golden pumpkin
With coachmen like rats?
A castle that sways
on an elephant's back?
A long, steamy train
Going clickety clack?
Or a ship with blue sails
And YOUR name on the side?
If YOU were a princess, what would YOU ride?

A selected list of titles available from Macmillan Children's Books

The prices shown below are correct at the time of going to press. However, Macmillan Publishers reserves the right to show new retail prices on covers, which may differ from those previously advertised.

Princess Poems
by Clare Bevan   978-0-330-43389-1   £3.99

Fairy Poems
by Clare Bevan   978-0-330-43352-5   £3.99

More Fairy Poems
by Clare Bevan   978-0-330-43935-0   £3.99

Crazy Mayonnaisy Mum
by Julia Donaldson   978-0-330-41490-6   £3.99

Ballerina Stories
chosen by Emma Young   978-0-330-45273-1   £4.99

All Pan Macmillan titles can be ordered from our website, www.panmacmillan.com, or from your local bookshop and are also available by post from:

Bookpost, PO Box 29, Douglas, Isle of Man IM99 1BQ
Credit cards accepted. For details:
Telephone: 01624 677237
Fax: 01624 670923
Email: bookshop@enterprise.net
www.bookpost.co.uk

Free postage and packing in the United Kingdom